REPEATABLE BACKGROUNDS
Fabric Weaves and Textures

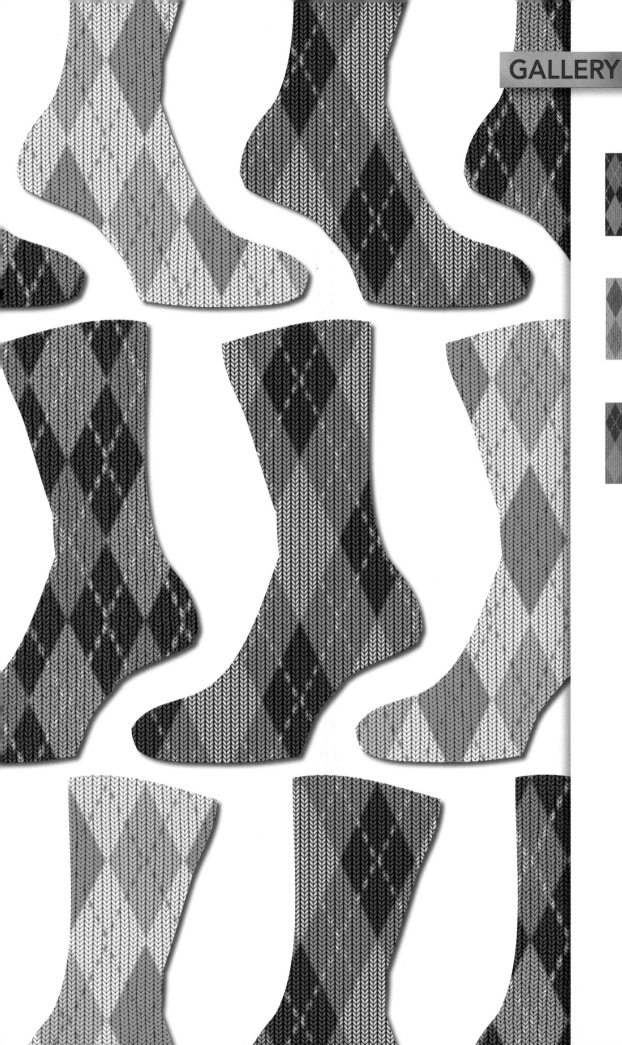

134

135

140

114

018

144

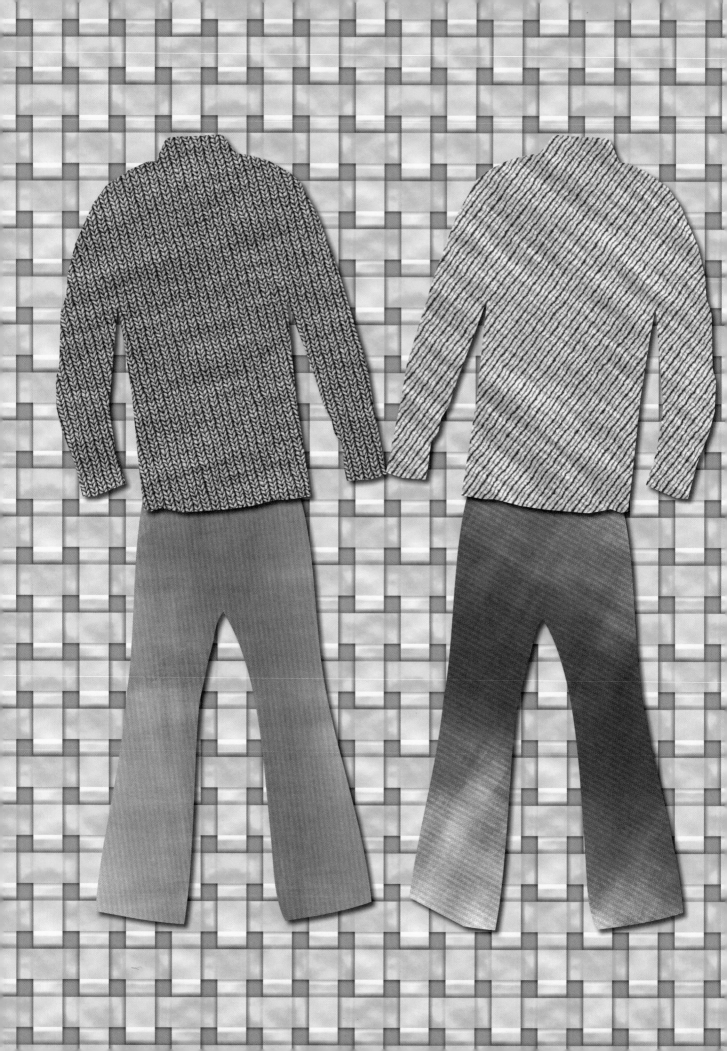

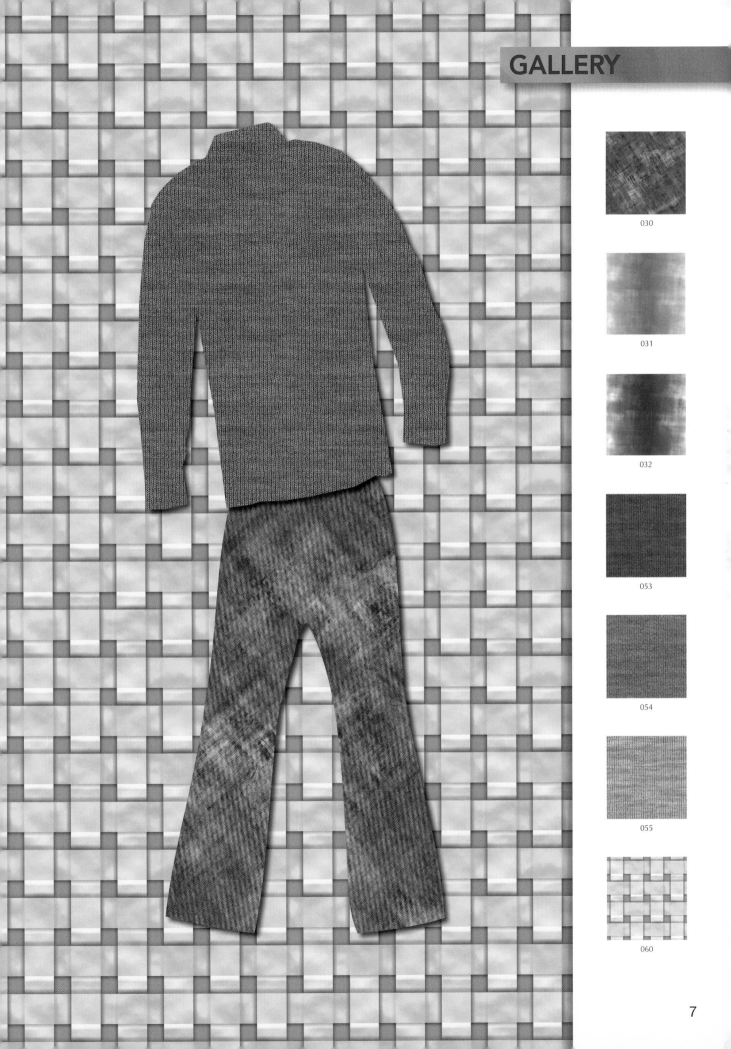

030

031

032

053

054

055

060

073

074

076

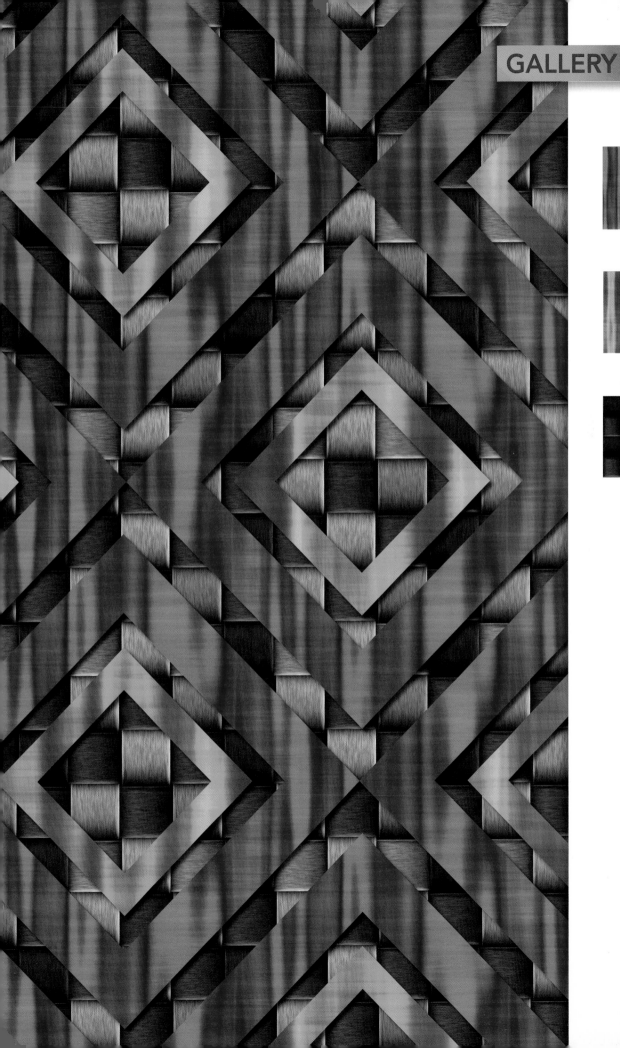

034

036

007

150

075

043

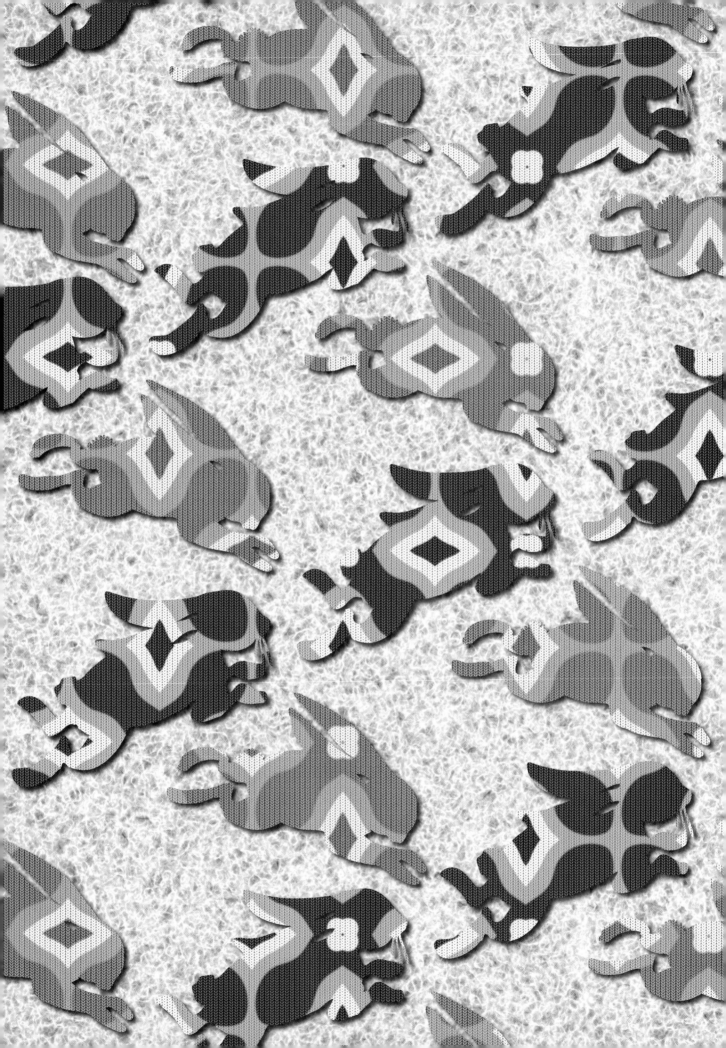

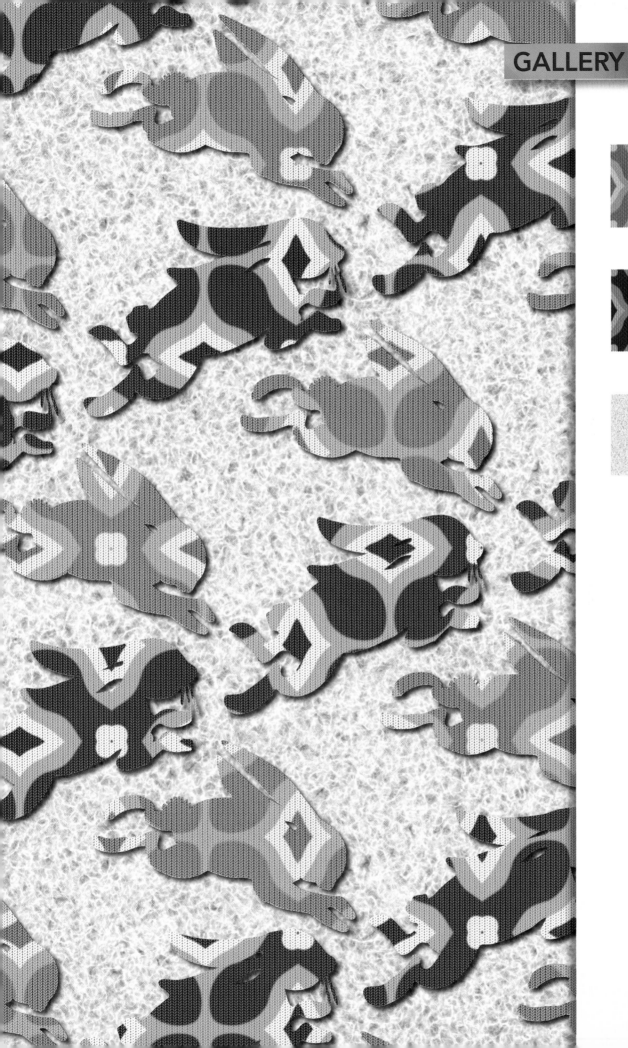

025

026

039

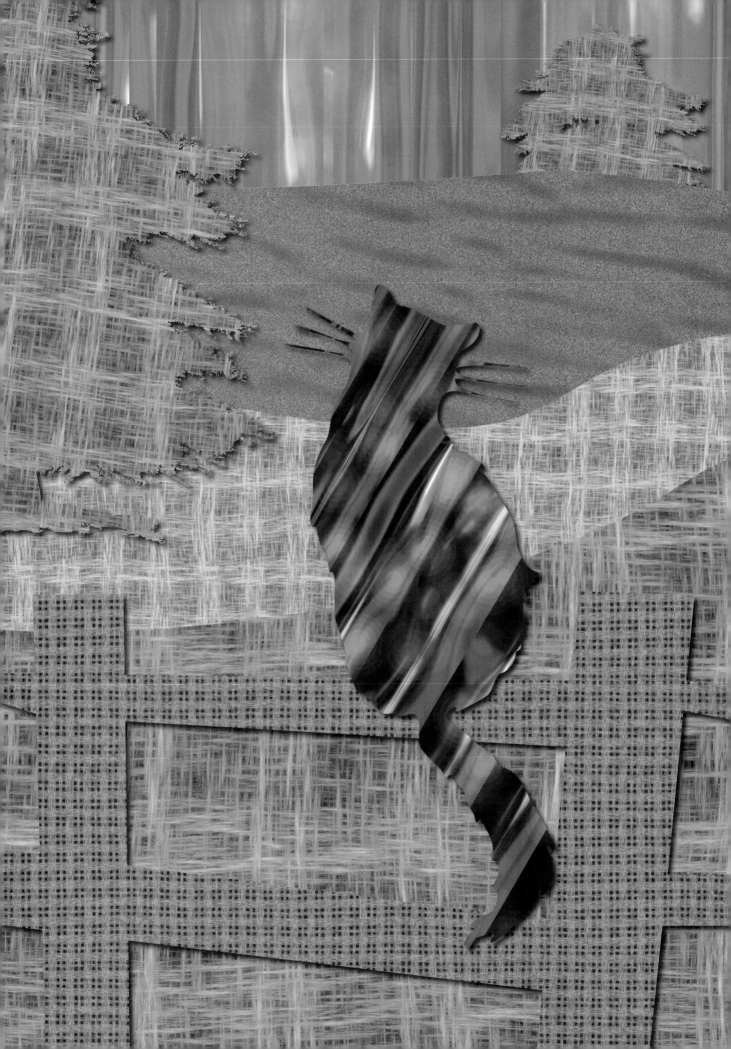

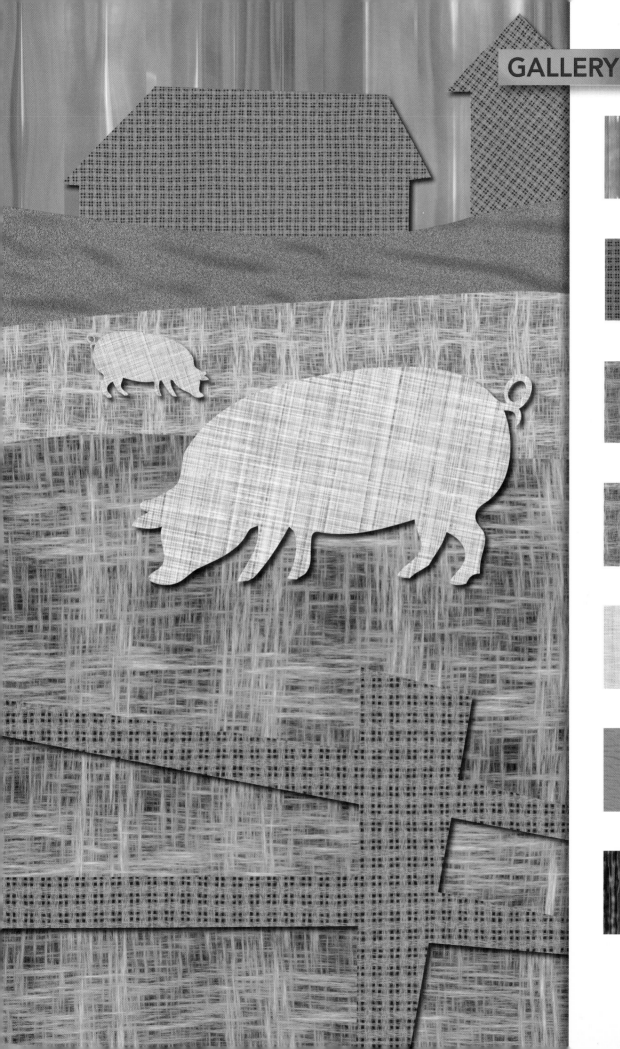

129

121

123

124

092

190

131

009

010

011

012

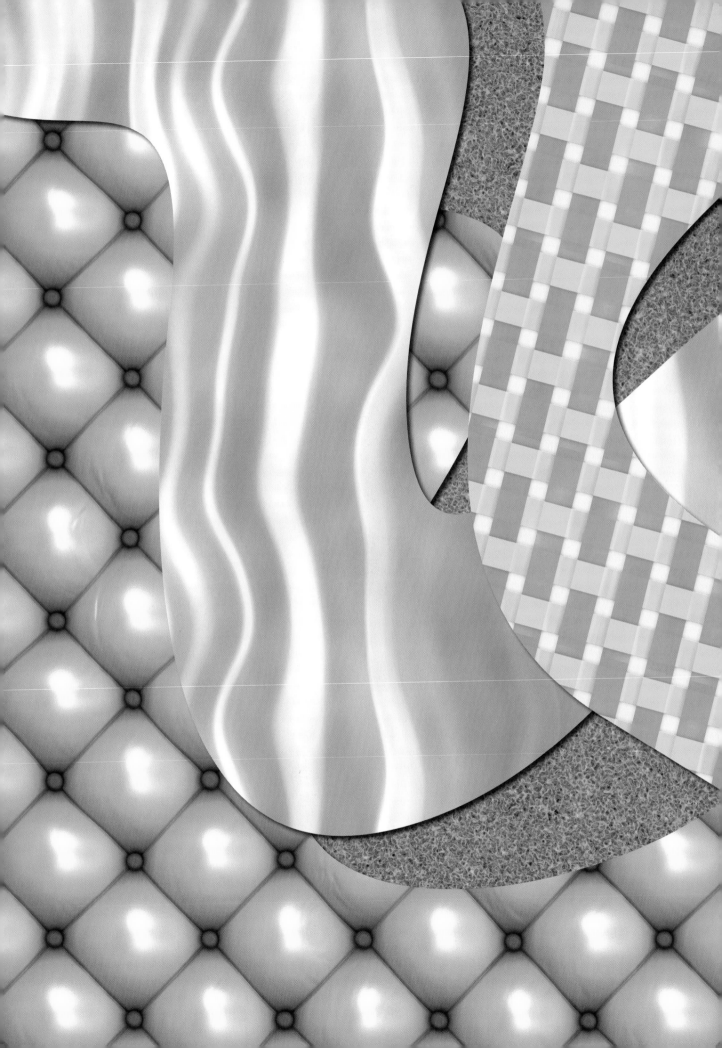

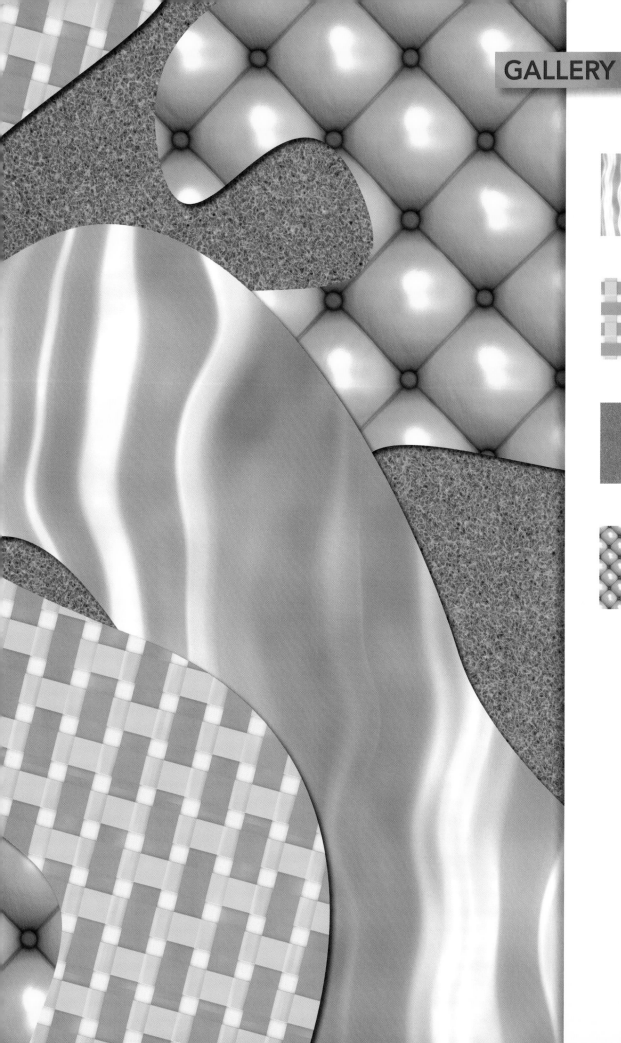

049

058

037

064

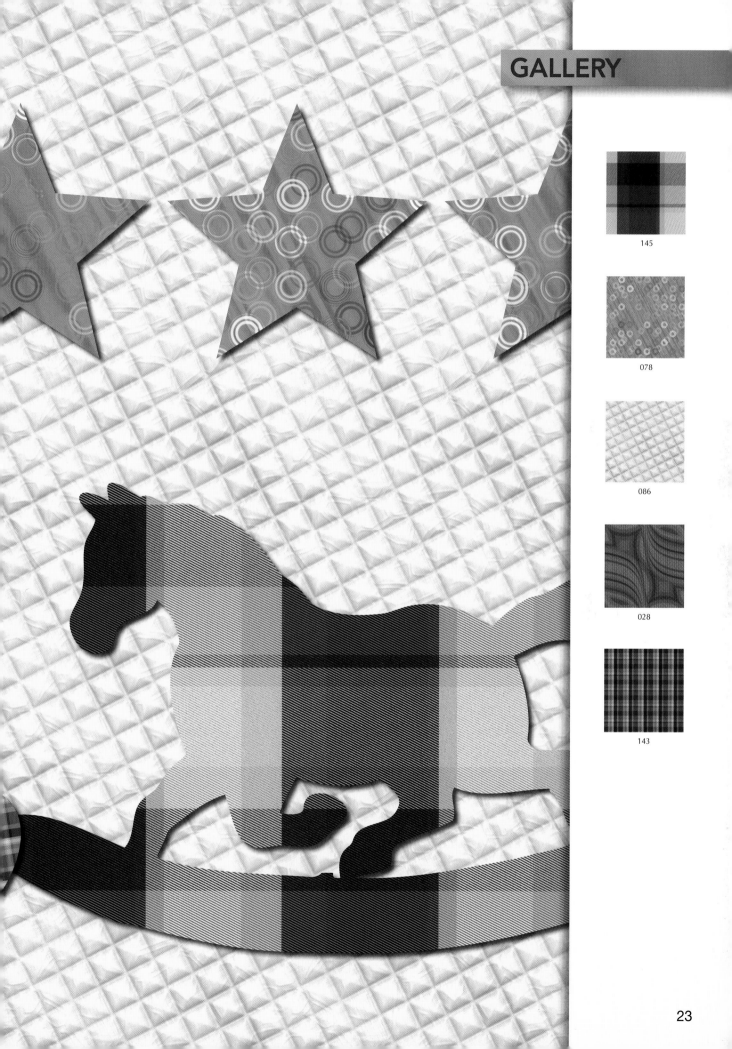

145

078

086

028

143

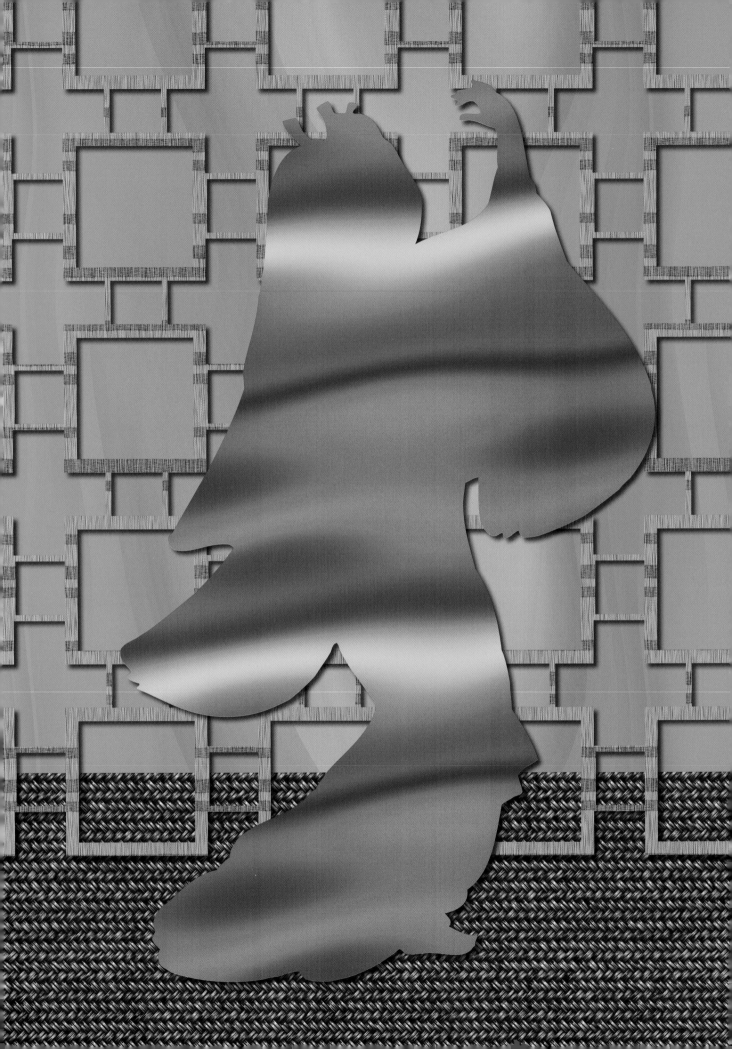

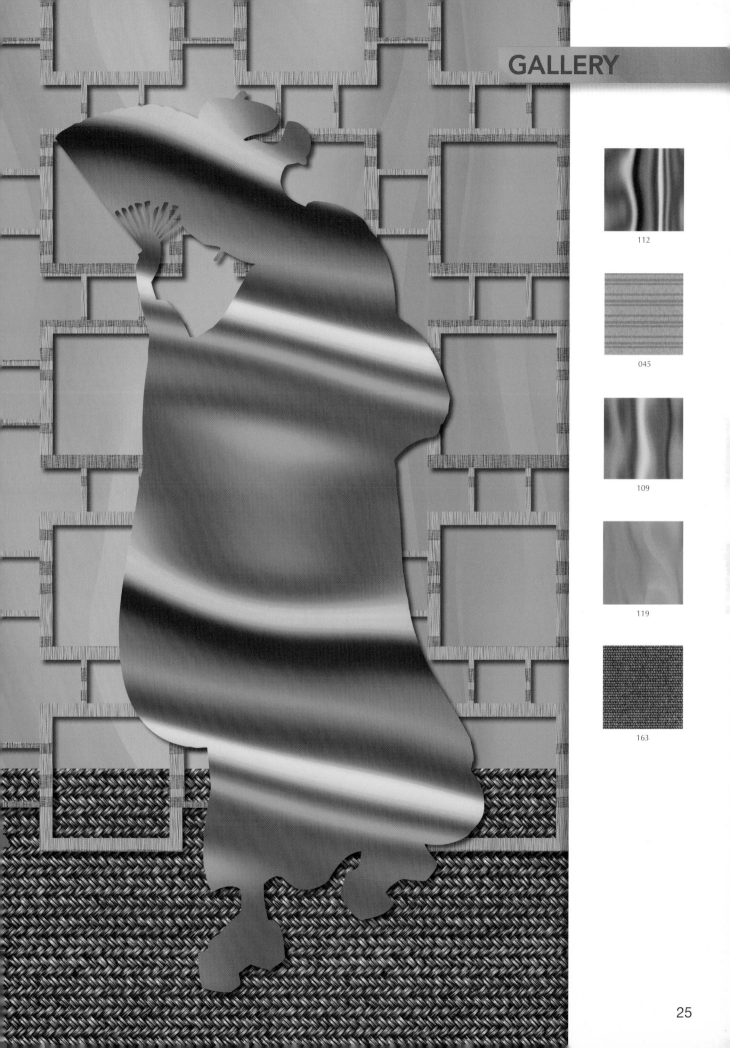

112

045

109

119

163

094

006

166

008

178

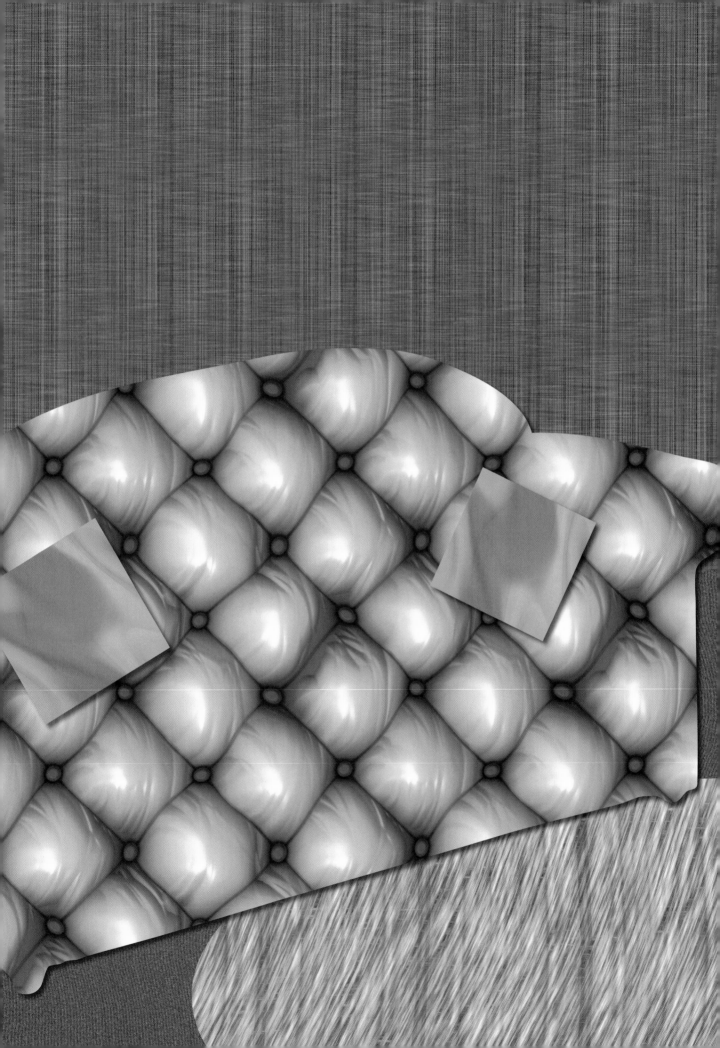

062

065

089

080

191

196

120

DESKTOP PICTURE

1

🍎 **Grab** File Edit Capture Window Help

About This Mac
Software Update…
Mac OS X Software…

System Preferences…
Dock ▶

Recent Items ▶

Force Quit… ⌥⌘⏏

Sleep
Restart…
Shut Down…

Log Out Alan Weller… ⇧⌘Q

Desktop Pattern for Mac.

1. Choose Apple > System Preferences.
2. From System Preferences Menu choose Desktop & Screen Saver.
3. In the Desktop & Screen Saver Menu be sure to click "Desktop" from the Desktop/Screen Saver button at top.

   Then click the plus sign found in lower left corner.
4. Locate the image from the pop-up menu then click the Choose button.
5. Then choose Tile from the pop-up selector located above the images.

30

Desktop Pattern for Windows.

1. Choose Start > Control Panel.
2. From the Control Panel Menu choose Display.
3. In the Display Properties Menu choose "Desktop" from the list of items at top.

   Then click the Browse Button.
4. In the Browse Menu find and select the image for the desktop pattern; then click the Open Button.
5. Back in the Display Properties Menu find your image in the "Backgrounds List," select it, then choose "Tile" from the Position Drop-down Menu. Finally, click the Apply Button, then the OK Button.

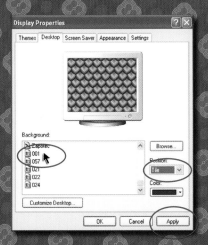

Creating a background pattern.

1. Create a new file or open a working one.
2. Choose Modify > Page Properties.
3. In the Page Properties Dialog box either type in a path to an image or click the Browse button to locate the image you are using to make a pattern.

   Note: Use the Web Ready images provided on the CD. These images are 72 dpi and optimized for internet use.
4. Then choose repeat from the Repeat pop-up menu.
5. Click Apply to preview the pattern (5) or choose OK to finish.

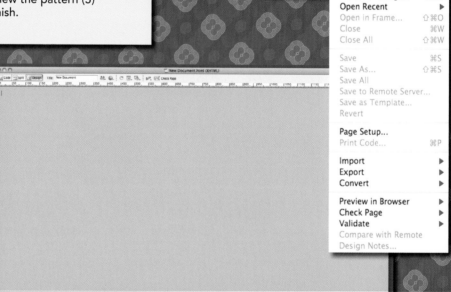

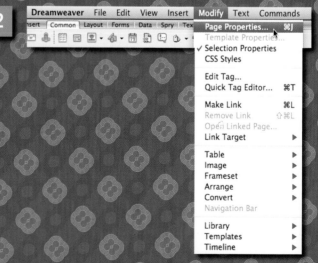

3

Page Properties

Category

Appearance
Links
Headings
Title/Encoding
Tracing Image

Appearance

Page font: Default Font **B** *I*

Size: pixels

Text color:

Background color:

Background image: Browse...

Repeat:

Margins

Left: pixels   Right: pixels

Top: pixels   Bottom: pixels

Help   Apply   Cancel   OK

4

Page Properties

Category

Appearance
Links
Headings
Title/Encoding
Tracing Image

Appearance

Page font: Default Font **B** *I*

Size: pixels

Text color:

Background color:

Background image: ../../../dw_sample.jpg Browse...

Repeat:
- repeat
- repeat-x
- repeat-y
- no-repeat

Margins

Left: pi...   Right: pixels

Top: pixels   Bottom: pixels

Help   Apply   Cancel   OK

5

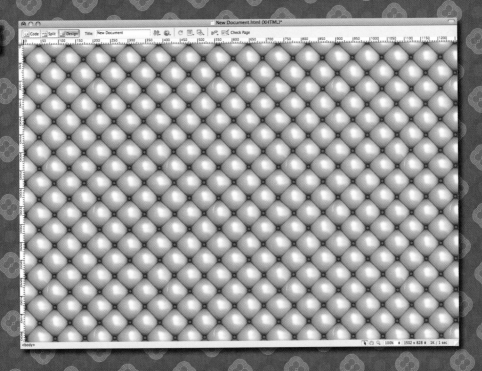

ADOBE ILLUSTRATOR

Turning an image into a fill pattern.

1. Open the file that you want to turn into a fill pattern.

2. Choose Select > All.

3. Choose Edit > Copy.

4. Create a new file or open a working one.

5. Choose Edit > Paste.

6. With the object still selected, Choose Edit > Define Pattern.

7. Enter a name for the pattern in the Pattern Name dialog box.

8. The pattern should show up in the Swatches Menu.

Filling a selection with the pattern.

9. Create a shape to fill with the pattern.

10. Select the shape using the Select Tool from the Tool Bar.

11. Then select the fill pattern from the Swatches Menu. The highlighted shape should fill with the selected pattern.

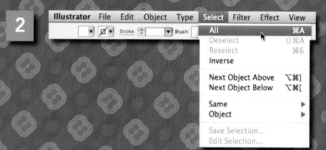

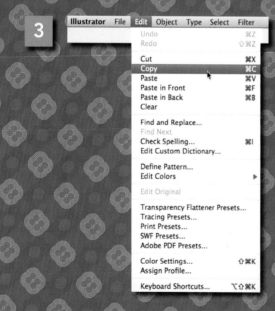

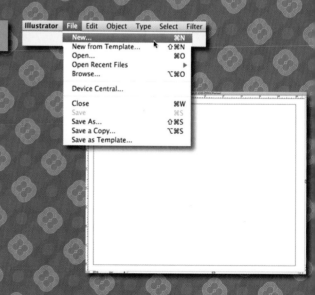

5

Illustrator	File	Edit	Object	Type	Select	Filter

Undo ⌘Z
Redo ⇧⌘Z

Cut ⌘X
Copy ⌘C
Paste ⌘V
Paste in Front ⌘F
Paste in Back ⌘B
Clear

Find and Replace...
Find Next
Check Spelling... ⌘I
Edit Custom Dictionary...

Define Pattern...
Edit Colors ▶

Edit Original

Transparency Flattener Presets...
Tracing Presets...
Print Presets...
SWF Presets...
Adobe PDF Presets...

Color Settings... ⇧⌘K
Assign Profile...

Keyboard Shortcuts... ⌥⇧⌘K

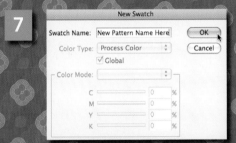

6

Illustrator	File	Edit	Object	Type	Select	Filter

Undo ⌘Z
Redo ⇧⌘Z

Cut ⌘X
Copy ⌘C
Paste ⌘V
Paste in Front ⌘F
Paste in Back ⌘B
Clear

Find and Replace...
Find Next
Check Spelling... ⌘I
Edit Custom Dictionary...

Define Pattern...
Edit Colors ▶

Edit Original

Transparency Flattener Presets...
Tracing Presets...
Print Presets...
SWF Presets...
Adobe PDF Presets...

Color Settings... ⇧⌘K
Assign Profile...

Keyboard Shortcuts... ⌥⇧⌘K

7

New Swatch

Swatch Name: New Pattern Name Here   OK

Color Type: Process Color   Cancel
☑ Global

Color Mode:

C ———————— 0 %
M ———————— 0 %
Y ———————— 0 %
K ———————— 0 %

8

Swatches ×

New Pattern

9

10

11

35

Making a Photoshop image into a pattern.

1. Open the file you want to create a pattern from.

2. Choose Select > All.

3. Choose Edit > Define Pattern.

4. Enter a name for the pattern in the Pattern Name dialog box.

Filling a selection with the pattern.

5. Create a new file or open a working one.

6. Select the layer or part of the image you want to fill.

7. Do one of the following:

   A. Select the Paint Bucket tool In the options bar, choose Pattern from the Fill pop-up menu, and select a pattern from the Pattern pop-up palette. Then click to fill the selected area with the pattern.

   B. Choose Edit > Fill. In the Fill dialog box, for Use, choose Pattern, select a pattern from the pop-up palette, and click OK. If Pattern is dimmed, you need to load a pattern library before you can select this option. (Not Illustrated)

1
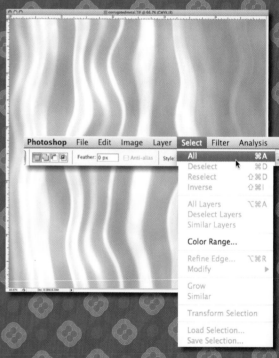

2
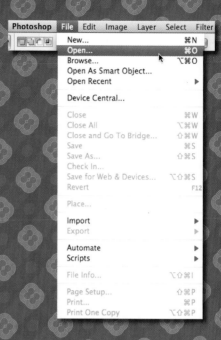

3
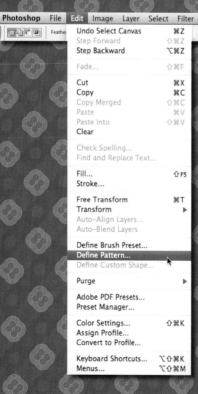

4

5

6

7-A

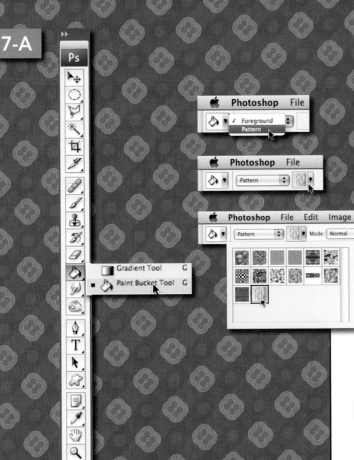

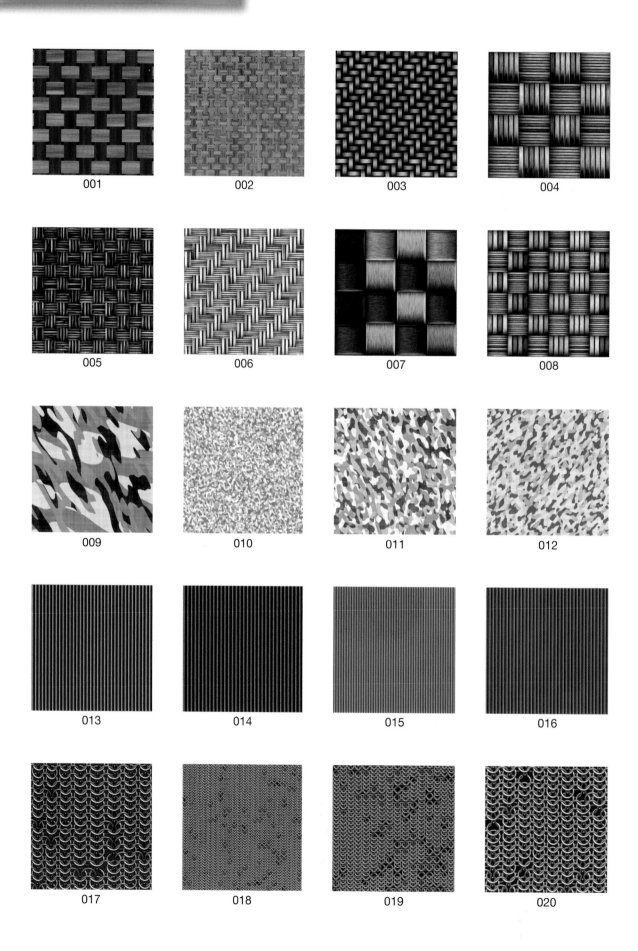

001

002

003

004

005

006

007

008

009

010

011

012

013

014

015

016

017

018

019

020

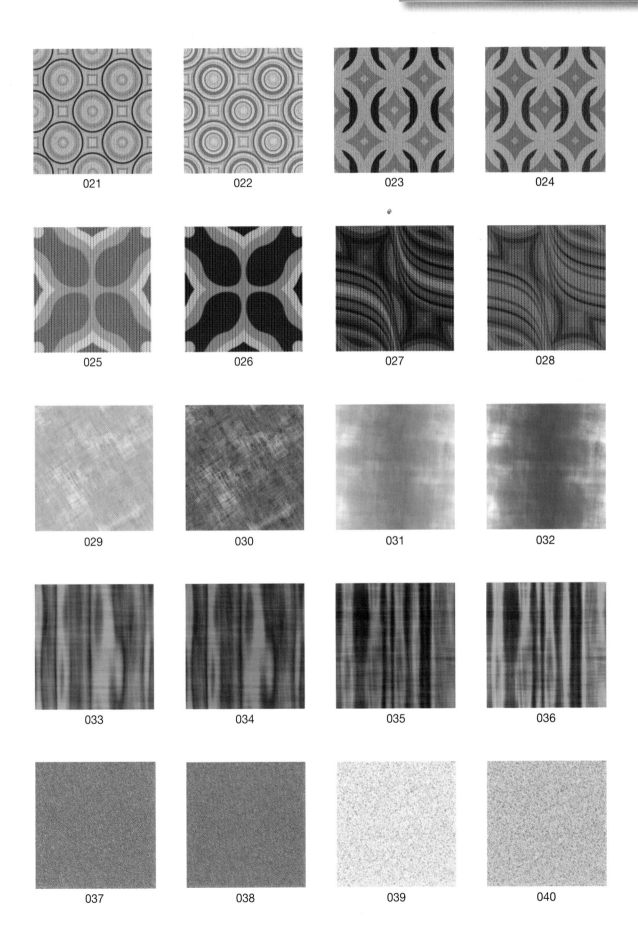

021

022

023

024

025

026

027

028

029

030

031

032

033

034

035

036

037

038

039

040

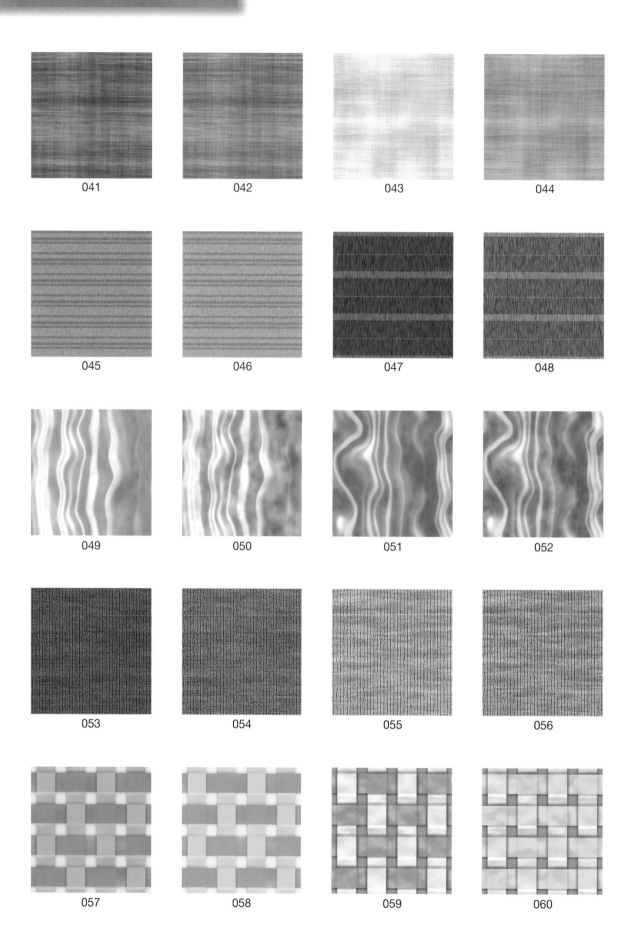

041

042

043

044

045

046

047

048

049

050

051

052

053

054

055

056

057

058

059

060

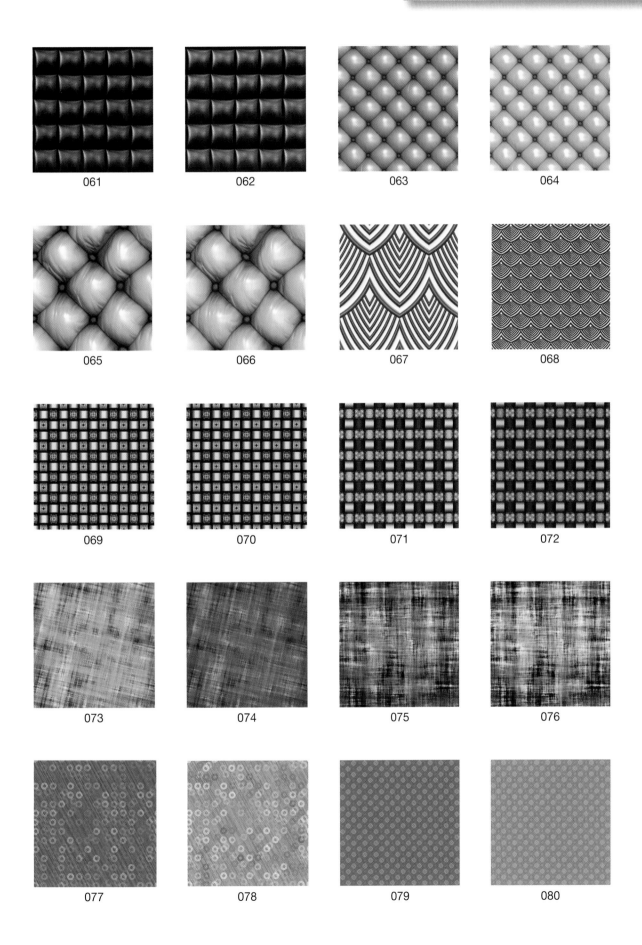

061

062

063

064

065

066

067

068

069

070

071

072

073

074

075

076

077

078

079

080

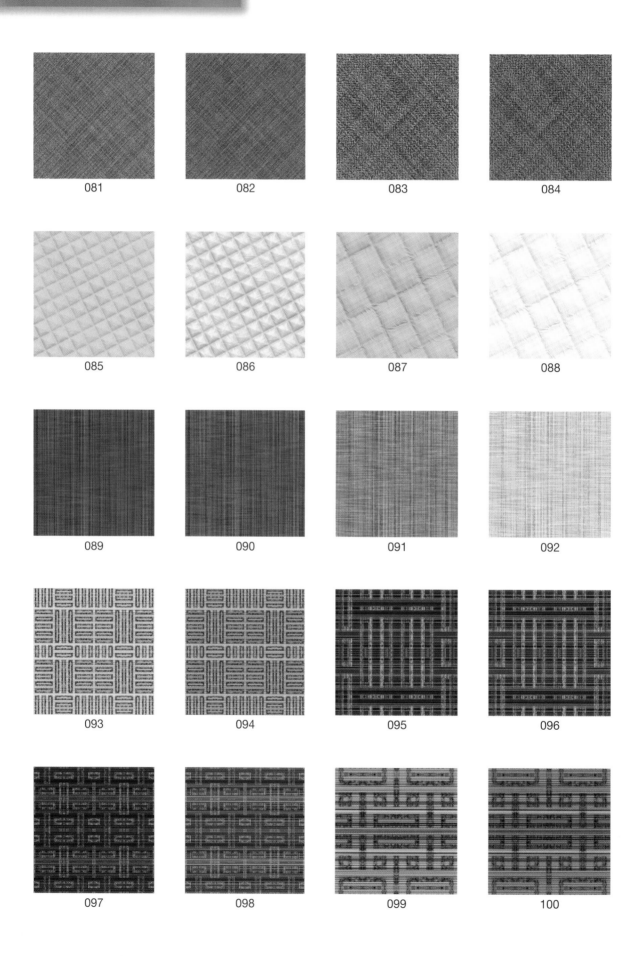

081

082

083

084

085

086

087

088

089

090

091

092

093

094

095

096

097

098

099

100

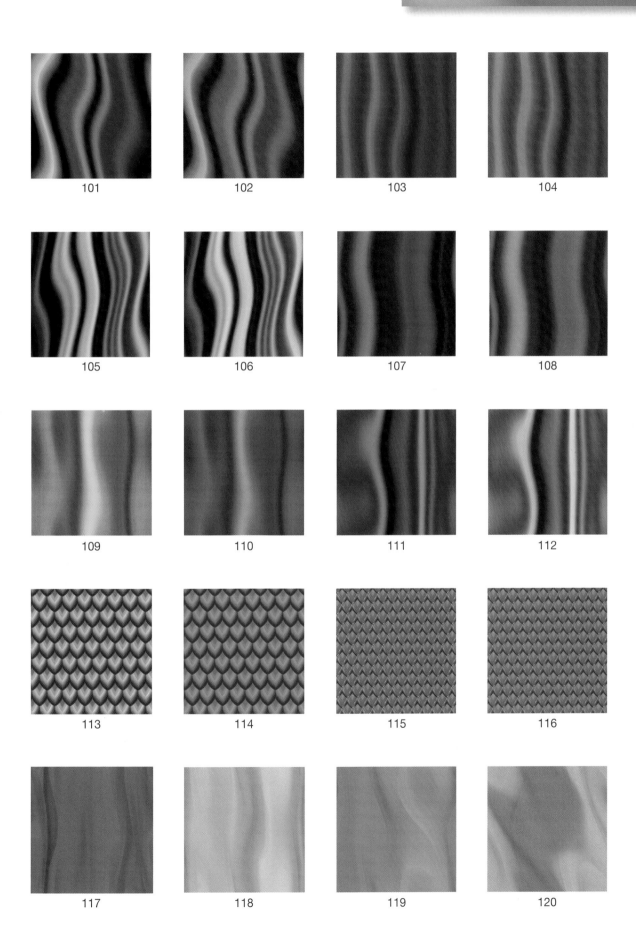

101

102

103

104

105

106

107

108

109

110

111

112

113

114

115

116

117

118

119

120

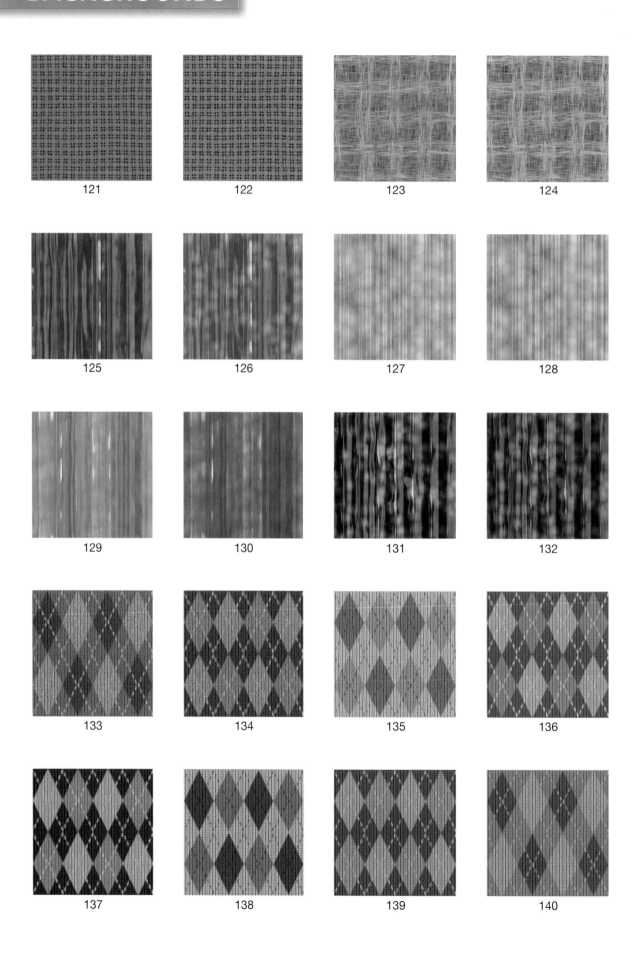

121 122 123 124

125 126 127 128

129 130 131 132

133 134 135 136

137 138 139 140

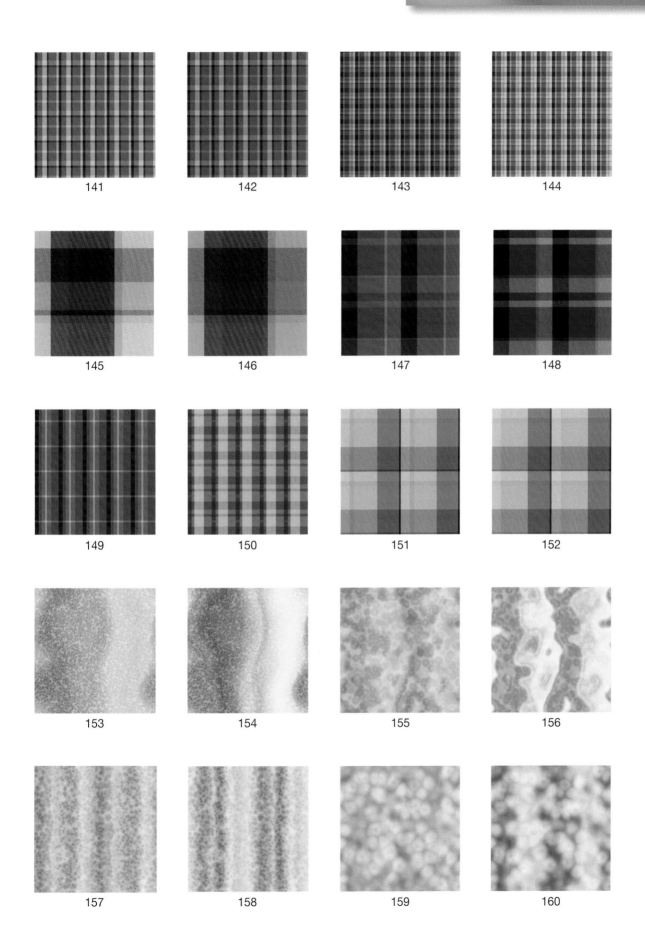

141

142

143

144

145

146

147

148

149

150

151

152

153

154

155

156

157

158

159

160

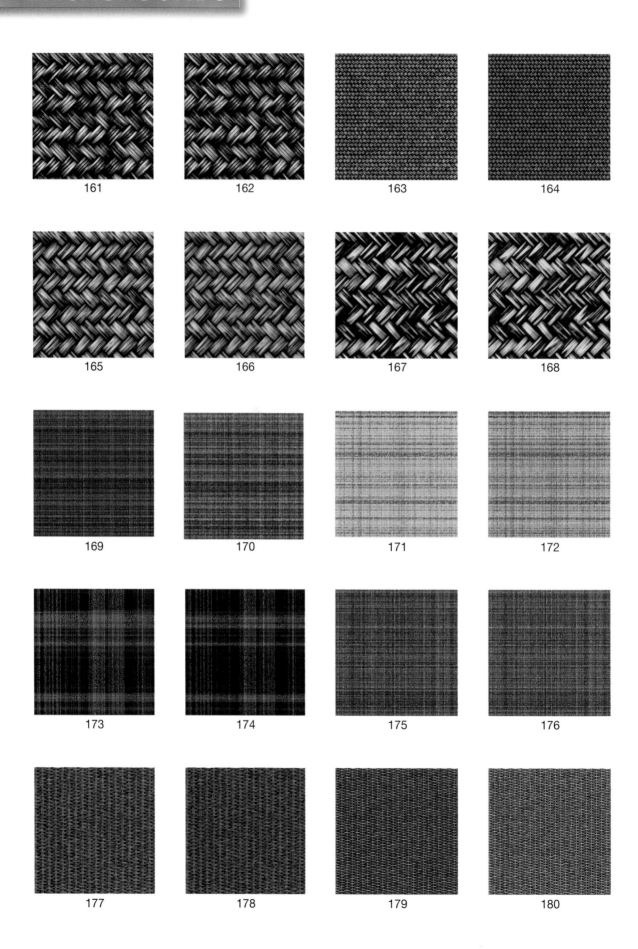

161 162 163 164

165 166 167 168

169 170 171 172

173 174 175 176

177 178 179 180

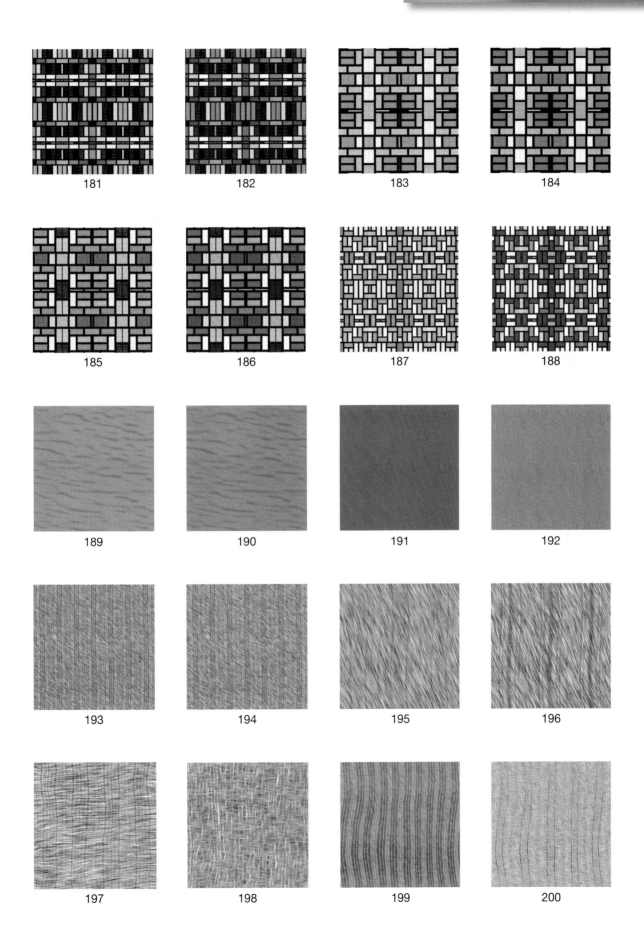

181   182   183   184

185   186   187   188

189   190   191   192

193   194   195   196

197   198   199   200